Farm An

Contents

Cows

cow

calf

Cows and their calves live in large fields. Cows eat grass and hay.

leather shoes

butter

beef

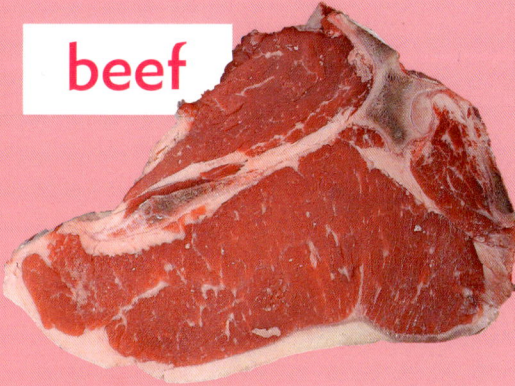

milk

We get milk, meat and leather from cows. Milk is made into butter, cheese and ice-cream.

Sheep

sheep

lamb

Sheep and their lambs live in large fields. Sheep eat grass and hay.

woollen hat and mittens

lamb

knitting wool

We get wool and meat from sheep. Wool can be made into clothes, blankets and carpet.

Goats

goat

kid

Goats and their kids live in fields. Goats eat grass and other plants.

goat's cheese

goat's skin

goat's wool

We get milk, meat, wool and leather from goats. Goat's milk can be made into cheese.

7

Chickens

hen

chicks

Hens and their chicks live in chicken coops. Chickens eat grains and other foods.

8

eggs

roast
chicken

We get eggs and meat
from chickens.

Ducks

duck

ducklings

Ducks and their ducklings live in duck coops. Ducks eat grains and other foods.

eggs

roast duck

We get eggs, meat and feathers from ducks. Duck feathers can be made into pillows and quilts.

Farm animals

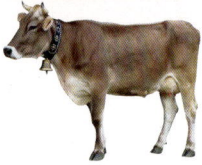 **cows**

 **sheep**

 **goats**

 **chickens**

 **ducks**